Reptilia

Reptilia

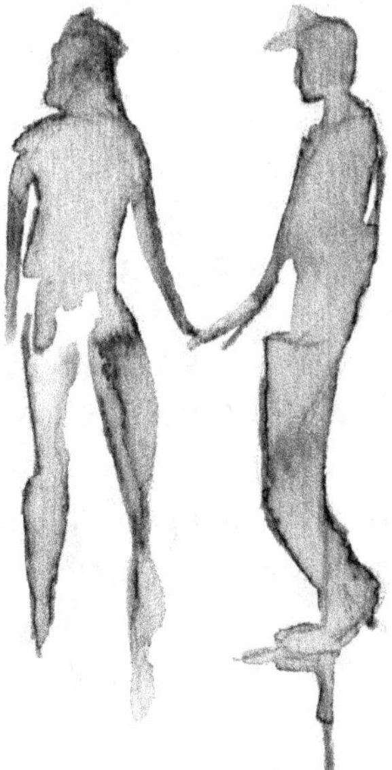

Hanna Tawater

Ayahuasca Publishing

Ayahuasca Publishing
3245 University Ave. Ste. 1430,
San Diego, CA 92104

Printed in the United States of America

First edition, 2018

Designed by Olivia M. Croom
Cover art & Illustrations by Laura Gwynne
Edited by Matt E. Lewis
Ayahuasca logo by Victoria Paul

ISBN-13: 978-0692065303
ISBN-10: 069206530X

ayahuascapublishing.com
@ayahuascapub
ayahuascapublishing
@ayahuascapub

Contents

This [it] finished off, making the surface smooth all around for many reasons; in the first place, because the living being had no need of eyes when there was nothing remaining outside [it] to be seen; nor of ears when there was nothing to be heard; and there was no surrounding atmosphere to be breathed; nor would there have been any use of organs by the help of which [it] might receive [its] food or get rid of what [it] had already digested, since there was nothing which went from [it] or came into [it]: for there was nothing beside [it]. Of design [it] was created thus, [its] own waste providing [its] own food, and all that [it] did or suffered taking place in and by [it]self.

—Plato, *Timaeus*

Shipwrights

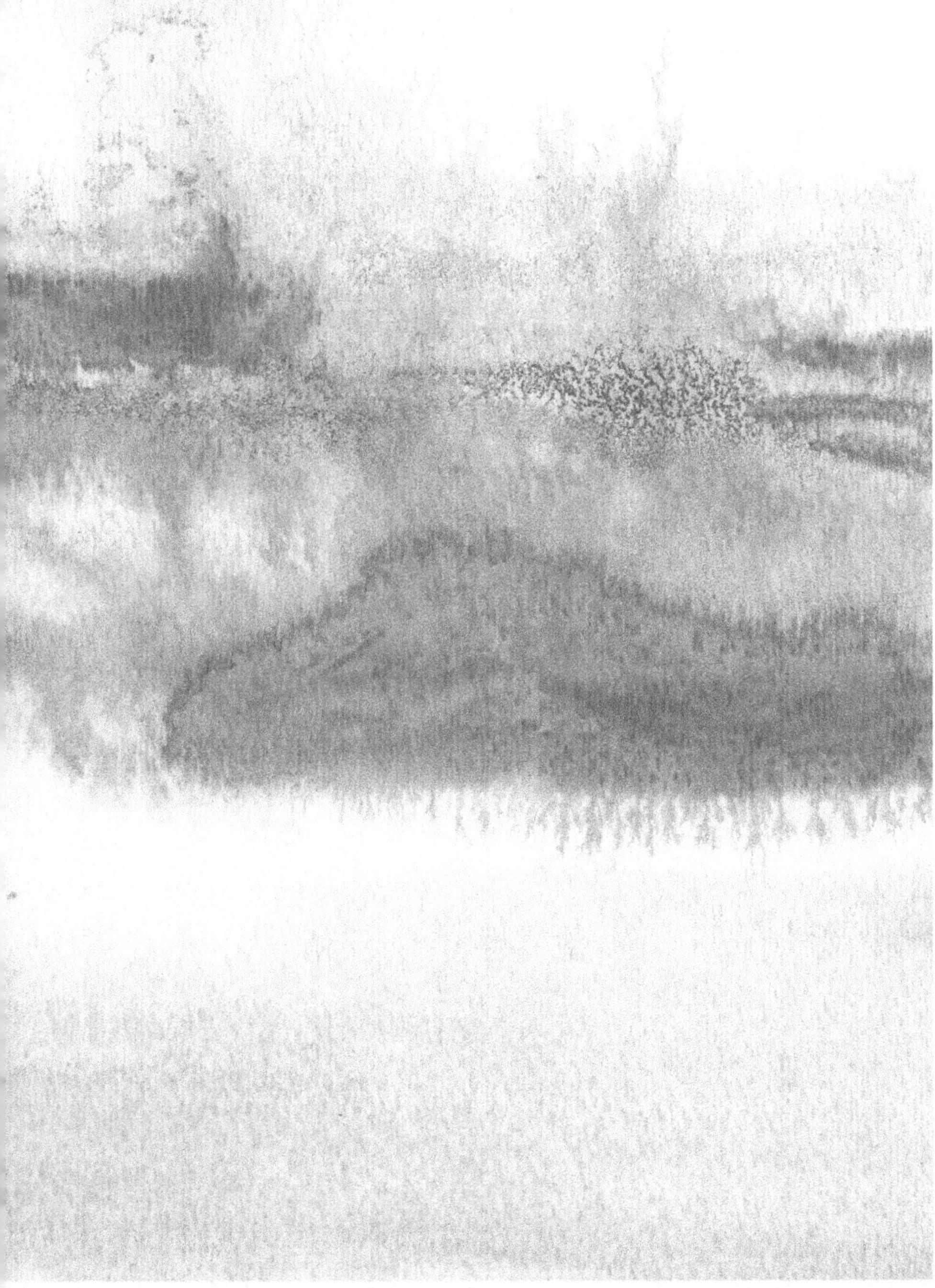

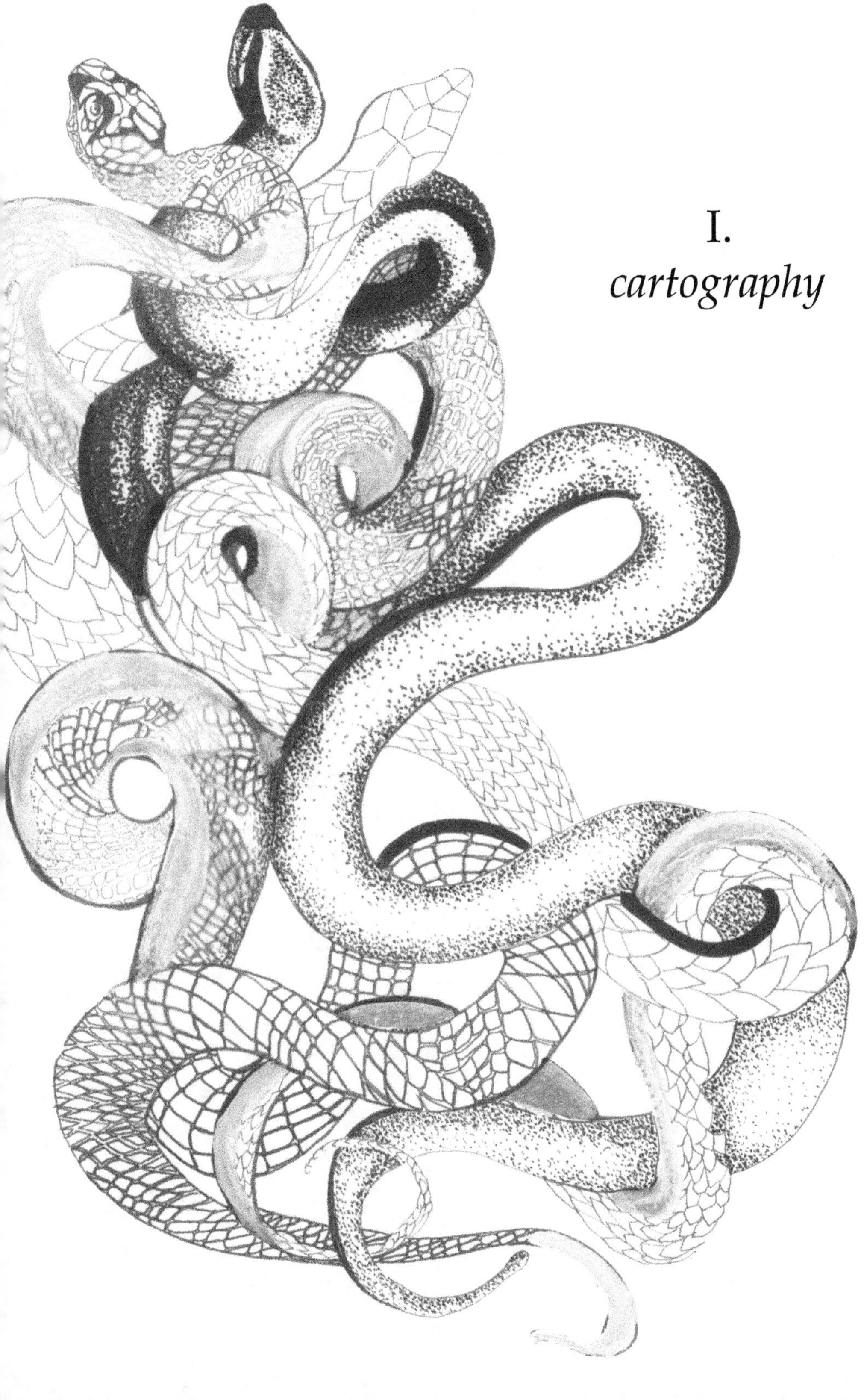

I.
cartography

Crotalinae

Fingertips possess the highest concentration of receptors and thermoreceptors in the body, second only to genitals. Imagine gesturing with your genitals. Stroking the surface of parchment with a phallus, grasping a pen with a vulva. Imagine feeling blind through blueprint with cock or cunt. Imagine eyeless wormy fingers dulled by comparison.

Some snakes can see heat, while we can only feel its vibration.

Typhlopidae

No, start with this

its tiny tail coiling around the tip-most phalange
bleeding toward the knuckle

it can flex, extend, circumduct its little tongue
you have options

you have a slender scaled black prehensility
you have nascent reptiles charred and writhing around
each digit

massaging at the reflexes.

~

start a stretch

its tiny body, an ulnic tendon really, extending to recoil
vibration against receptors clustered
responding to a whisper, a hot puff of breath, a flick of a forked tongue

slaver pooling down the divot between thumb and index

a small necrotic scaphoid fracturing the creases
the twist of phantom appendages
once engaging in fine manipulation with the forelimb

but you were caught between page and wrist

you have a backspace
you have a bruised serpentine hollow

you have localized tenderness within the snuffbox

~

start again

try it this time with the lens stretched
moving back and forth across the retina
try it this time with the residue sloughed off
a vellum too taut for gesticulation

you have options

Hydrophiinae

slither an undercurrent
humped protrusions

unlabeled archipelago
snaking through a pool

of spilt ink

on a map

joints breaking
through opaque
glassy surface somewhere

before the continental shift

ridges at the edges of the trench
where blind worms feed on sulfide

pelagic layers of pressure
overlapping
nutrient bodies
water like obsidian scales

one long muscle making
letters in sand

Acrochordidae

sailed a shore jotting
every nook and inlet

once I saw a tree
grasping an edge
and blotted out
by a drip

once I saw the perimeter
and turned my sails back-
ward brushing under
belly to the hull

Aniliidae

Q: What do a geographer, a painter, and a technician have in common?
Q: Are we general or thematic?

~

Rattlesnake
Death Adder
Saw Scaled and Chain Vipers
Philippine Cobra
Tiger Snake
Black Mamba
Taipan and Fierce
Blue Krait
Eastern Brown
Belcher's Sea

~

A: a map of lung, liver
A: long singular muscles
A: cross-hatched, charted
A: linked across four arrows

~

a scale
a bent back fang
toward a throat

a vestigial nib
etching a signature
along a fjord

~

cartography is reality
remolded to speak spatial
resonance
in accordance with—

Elapidae

start here

pretty in aphasia while I finish
this topographical map
sketch each fold
shade each crest
add a rose pointing
toward the temporal lobe
where the venom bled / panthalassic /
in one paralyzing perimeter

thirty feet wrapped around the critical period
pressure against its pretty neck

embellished along the border
entrapment of a median nerve

~

even a sea monster
painted mythos
stretched and slender
compassed around each quadrant

a stunted neuroplasticity
stagnating skin hollowed
crumpled mute and senseless
condensing wave to stasis
more easily digested

it's only neuropathy and even numb fingers can still curl
scratching along gridlines

~

have a head start

write each word you remember
I'll pierce them with a vibration
stick my little tongue into each one
and lap at air

while I think of something better

to say

and compose a map of metaphors
for poisoned speech
a red-faced cloud blowing curlicues from the upper
corner into paper sails

~

snake around each finger
knuckle to the fibers kneading
threading belly to the current
rewritten taut and torn
until it's just a scrap
forced into glass

Anguidae

match struck against
faded parchment stained
spreading out in fingers
through thread

curled along edges
floating ashy
scales into a north
eastern wind
pulling towards sand

once I could have turned
sails back towards more
even horizons

once I could have colored over
mistakes in the design
an exaggerated tree
forgotten mass becoming less
pangaeaic drifting further
further off the border

once I could contain
a world on a piece of cloth

and burned away with the tiniest
lick of a forked flame

Xenopeltidae

we washed in an island
no names on our tongues
licking at salt

we waited in the sun to catch
a glimmer of movement
the juices drying
on our fingertips
the scales thinning
flaking papery, westward

II.
iconography

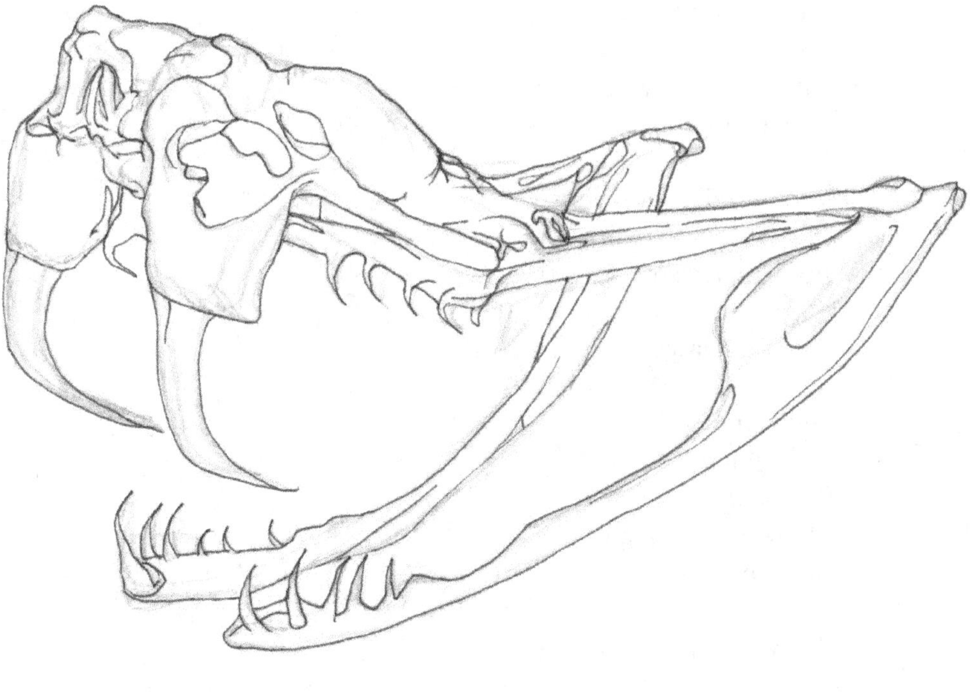

Ouroboros

start now
pigeonholed folding

in on itself

swallowing my own
alchemy - acid
dissolving tongue-tipped and cute
cued, the tip
my tongue sensorium

a museum

peepholed and shedding
into my own throat

skin that was always there
skein on the surface

with the tail lazily dipped
into netherworld, my mouth
impregnated small
gurgle in a pool
burst and gaseous

anima mundi
kundalini force
eternal return
my own mythologies
father, own

always/only just this one:

Nāgī

cutting currents a signature
essed down the Mekong
holding that entire
world-balanced on your snout
hoard of scales in your belly
you fireball breaking glass
leaning against a wet roof
top heavy father and laying clutches
in sand finned ribbon tracing waves
grasped and plucked
petal tied knotted
enclosed around a rod
iron pull fish-hooked
squirming and just hanging
there dripped in white
slipping from a dark slit
eggs erupted against wood
small gods
faded stains jaundice edging on
a timeless pinup

Nāga Vasuki

thin string in the center
of an inter-dimensional palm
tugging up a tuft of primordial
aluminum a trans-
human topography churning
in a cosmic ocean an opening
at the bottom of a whirl
pooling mercury G-
forcing into form an elemental
taking on light years in
directional aging in
the fifth sea

stretch an arm across one
universal, ancient soup
fat of the surface solidifying
into circuitry, serpentine
coiling blue around a throat
full of diesel, a crude nectar
dripping from the turning rod
onto dry basalt

Nāga Sesha

pick and plant
a green scab
for you, father I
still bleed minutes
and eons
nebulae dislodged
from under a crooked
platelet of an im-
material cosmo
snuggled in the hood
ticking, the corner of
an impostured king
cuddled in cold-
blooded rhythm
string vibrating
under your belly
a fourth dimension where
I rouse bearded and older
dividing into a left
over pile of spacedust
inching along your back
comfortable hoping
you don't recoil

Nāga Mucalinda

1. a parasite in the crease where hood meets neck

2. a necking under a tree of snakes

3. a snaking seven times around my gut

4. a gutting of a three-eyed milk fish

5. a fishing smoke in my wet clutch

6. a clutching of coils around a thin tongue

7. a tonguing at the crease where neck meets fang

it rained seven days
but I was cocooned with a cobra
head around each leg beneath a billowing
sheet sponging venom from parted
mouth unhinging at the jaw
swallowing it all bones and everything

I'm still missing one thing

Ningishzida

just only one
thirds man a cuff
off the shoulder
a staff in the belly
the bitch snake twining
around the other two
thirds god or goddess or
therioceph forked
in the tongue coughing
keratin in the belly
the inner core sulfuric
burp in the continuum
or maybe we were reversed
anthrocephs writhing below
the neck bottled into
furry quadrupedal grunts
clawing a cloying mark against
the good tree on a waterless
river barge wrung
on empty vessels bobbing
up and under currents
of static and hellfire

Wadjet - Renenutet - Nehebkau

1.
double headed, again, sides on the same
plane how can we be dia-
metric splash of *dasein* on the wind
shield unfastened in the collision
two heads are better
than two arms, fierce and with
more bite a shudder in the after
taste, scaly arc over the under
worldmaking and redisunconcealed

2.
harvest breeds war with the nile
makes it swell and overflow
into more fertile soil ploughed
molded into mud walls
a crust on the outer husk
a cobra on the crown relaxed
limp slaughter by gaze

3.
king or woman
in childbirth two
ladies, a snake with feathers
string around a circle
semisphere with a gilded
crest for every name scales
and feathers are made of the same
things, a gullet loose
enough to fit the sun
swallow coiled around a head
or shaft or arm of spiraling
light and radiation tiny explosions
cosmic lady of flame
soundless
I have et

but how can I mean, father
in this perpetual sameness
how can I mean, father, when
snakes are birds

The Coatls
(Quetzalcoatl, Mixcoatl, Coatlicue)

serpent and twin both
interlacing loop the continuum
vacuum swallowing whole
fucking planets, the harvest, star eater
plume of multicolored gasses
sprouting quill by quill by quill
down my neck of scales

1. feathered

my god of wind current wriggling
through light years turn in the middle
bending back towards venus embodiment
of sky sun fable my conquistador vision
underworlds seeing strange
sails on horizon father of fertility
my morningstar snake heart in beaked mask

2. cloud

war/ always/ and the hunt eating hearts
stars made out of proteins, aminos
smoke river taste, nuclear rich
harvest across ashes, dust, ancient light
all of this into one, father, with his bow
drawn behind a darker matter

3. mother of gods

my mother of war/ again/
chasing up skirts of serpents
back inside dense mass pushed out
stars moons everything a man
fully armed tosses heads
upwards becoming satellites an orbit
tracing magnetic to the one who devours
everything a ball of feathers ruptured
on my belly swollen my chain of hearts falling
from my headless neck gushed hatchlings –

father—this is how we birth

Hydra, Ophion, and the Gorgons

fucked an ocean wrapped seven times
around a bird, an egg, a hatchling in sand
I hoisted heaven against time, father
fighting minutes, fighting directionality
women with tails morphing into doves
blood so poisonous whole planets formed
in the space between words between ions
this madness growing two more in place
each second dividing in half ad infinitum
each inch until we never touch
slowing the rhythm of flightless titans
snakes mouthing underworlds
incubate other gods' spawn
hang constellated in star clusters
each severed line doubling chthonic or cosmic
divided twice more into stone, sea daughter,
changing gold into serpents with too many
heads to count so say just one
set of vacant eyes, eventual dust
eventual neutrinos slowed to apathy
sluggish and waiting for reaction, father waiting
for catalyst, eruption, a shift in the geography

Níðhöggr & Jörmungandr

tucked in wing
the end of all gnawing
the roots of corpses the world
tree sucking up carbon gnashing
teeth on the last great expulsion
malice and villain beasts root
forth from a gnarled
twisted thing with feathers

---

sea tail, a thread grasping
the other
side world tightening
a continuous recoiling
everything and all points
in time move across one sea
child, back-keeping
the minims strung together
until the moment I rise, fathered
from the ocean to poison
the sky in half notes and acid
single tone vibrating
a hall of twisted spines
endless ribs from which to choose
a newer species

Rainbow Serpent

has anyone else
made this
connecting patterns on the back
the beast with a lazy leg
dangling over the edge
like we were in a fucking psytrance
or something and the edge
of the infinite reached *us*
a common deity if creator
arcing over one pool to
another mirror over Charn
a wood between worlds
charred afterglowing portal
everywhen mythologies prism
in a dried dying capitol
slow decay of colored glass
uranic war waking ancient
unstable gods bleeding between
legs radioactive and ceremonial
half-lives
gassing race to arms
stretching from either end
blasting outwards fingertips
dipping into alternate dimensions
of the same fable I can't
be the only one who's here, father,
slowly decaying across spacetime

Ayida & Damballah

coiled seven-thousand times to keep from sinking
cosmic trench down through otherside into sky
and breath gushing blood into every ocean he took
another snakewife tightening around continents un-
til they split open newer mythologies other patterns
on more twisted bellies more gaseous nebulae
drifting into a newer symmetry - balance - father, I'm
falling through her coiled so close falling past all
thousands of lines stacked again and again and
again you are sky, cosmos, creator and here is a
newer ecology where even air is a snake womb
star forming cocoon of ions charges attracting
repelling pushing further from the other pole
eating my own tail my own waste keeping every
thing too heavy hovered in time in immaculate
minutes until a newer goddess and with less
burden it's so hard holding planets inside me
it's so hard being the only one who's here
hard being here only
hard being
who's here
who is here

Snake Dance

striking electric through sacred
static grounds passing side-
winding currents from multi
colored clouds a head
with feathers protruding
from a burrow, a metal
tube shooting messages skyward
coreward down through ore
and ash a dance erupting
middle of a different gorge
another plain, the rhythm
of time, circle swallowing
its end eternally recurring a wave
bouncing back
and forth between rocks
slipping into new skin
taking two snakewives bearing
serpentine children darting
naked and shouting
for rain for rain for rain

Odette

porte-bonhuer - small green
lizard from an African palm
it is to you, father, I owe emeralds

eyes in an asp twine around tiny
hands Cleopatra in the Coliseum
a lady cobra dancing a round waist

an asp on the tongue licks at royalties
feathers, jewels dripping from the neck
the medusa rhythm worthy
of blindness of execution
—by venom least terrible
ways to die, she said
destitute with too many
lovers in the bloodstream
heavy and heavier

a handsome woman
on stage with two
asps around the arms
stretching across the crowd
eight feet into dark
materializing a beat
against an hour
too late and everyone's
gone a lone striking woman
shimmying fathered into feathered skin

Caduceus

we're alchemic again
changing snakes into women
things with feathers two
heads entwined around great wooden
rod dipped mercurial
pool non-sticking
we're metals again
shape-shifting crime
fighting shepherds for
the flock the flight
of wingless birds
on raw bellies breathing
fire breathing war
breathing starting over
a roar across black pastures
heralding a boy too close
to the sun too green
for planting too volatile
to be molded only good
for knowing when
the weather will change

The Ophites

1. the light was the serpent
2. the serpent was the intellect
3. the intellect was the woman
4. the woman was the serpent
5. the serpent was the light
6. the light was the woman
7. the woman was the water
8. the water was the chaos
9. the chaos was the darkness
10. the darkness was the serpent
11. the serpent was the woman
12. the woman was the abyss
13. the abyss was staring, thrusting, erupting
into the dialectic the dia-
logos of havoc and harvest
an older woman bleeding still
always/ always/ iron into soil washing
vestigial feet molten and cooling into
a newer fable limbless and circling
a heavier mass folding under pressure one prismatic
diamond child only everything/ everything/
in this rightnow everywhen
I am the black hole birthing backwards
unfolded aminos
piecing my paper shell tighter from
inside where gold we change into
a brighter alloy
a more malleable metal

Ouroboros

start here
a slip inside
astride, a lick
a flickering astral
I am Mehen, father,
uncoiled and without
feet, always here forever
and been only
mhn and mthr
only here is all reused
points - möbius
terra formed and looped
I am the *prima materia*
and here is now
always only just starting over:

(or, how we looked for form)

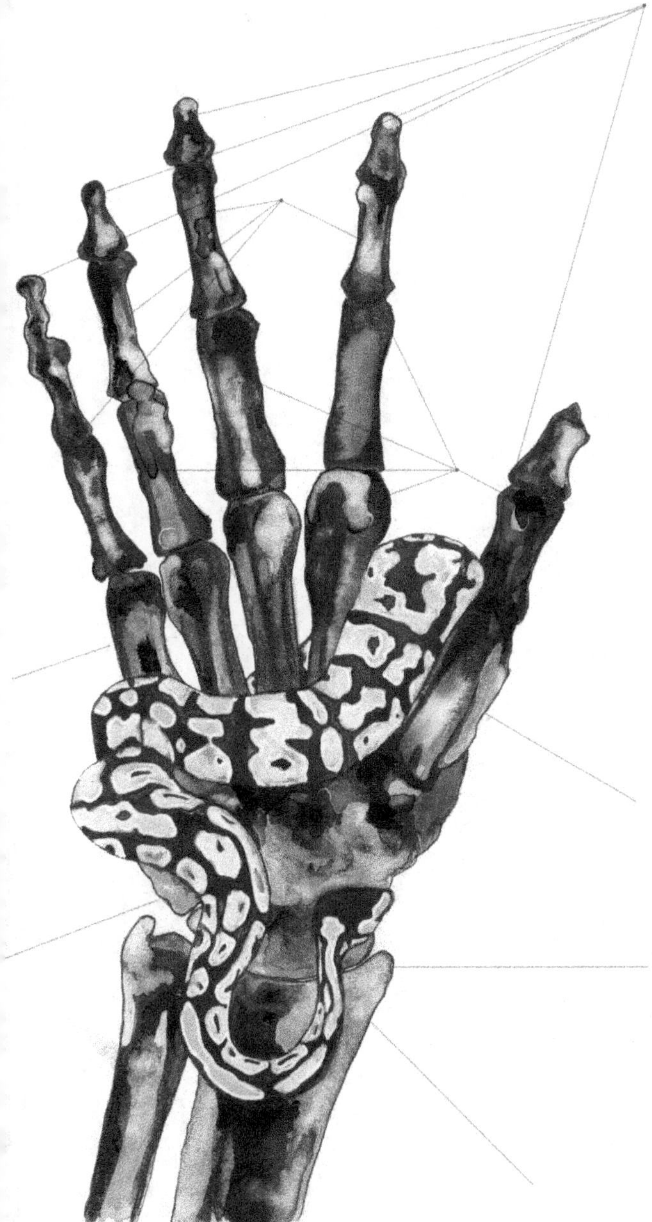

I.

Non-count nouns
(or, how we began to breathe)

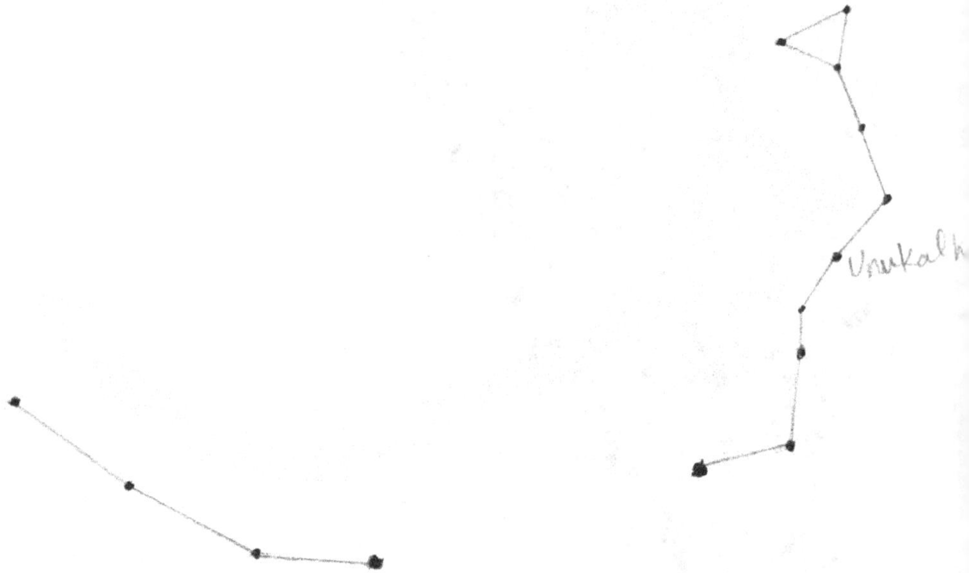

"all configurations which have previously
existed on this earth must yet meet, attract,
repulse, kiss, and corrupt each other again"

things in time

[sugar
[milk
[honey

concrete bodies

flat projection

epidermic space
may indeed disperse
(finite nitrates)

holographic discrete
sequences

[I was polyatomic and soluble]

recursion of numbness
hovering baubles
bawdy isomorphous

lust]
heat]
hydrogen]

a morphism
again

recurrence of
the smallest
particles
splitting

dispersion
atoms with determinate
numbers

afeeling, cold digits tracing

downward in points

pinned pricked

stymied motionless
equating protuberance on a line
graphed direct path

long according
eternal laws governing

we govern

the numbness
of infinite projection

combinations
eternal play

multifoliate
repetition

[you governed skin]
[meant skin]
[skin-kissed

I gaped
I gasped]

recombinant gaps
culminating the devolution
synoptic amorphous uncoiling
disordering taxonomical
subversion disordered occurrence
excerpts disorder the ions
holographic static disruption
erupting polarized repulsions
disorder the order of
sequence compounding proto noise
typical combustions disjuncting
the bonds

the space

propelling

between

synapses

and we do disperse
like observed photons

II.
Particles
(or, how we came to be)

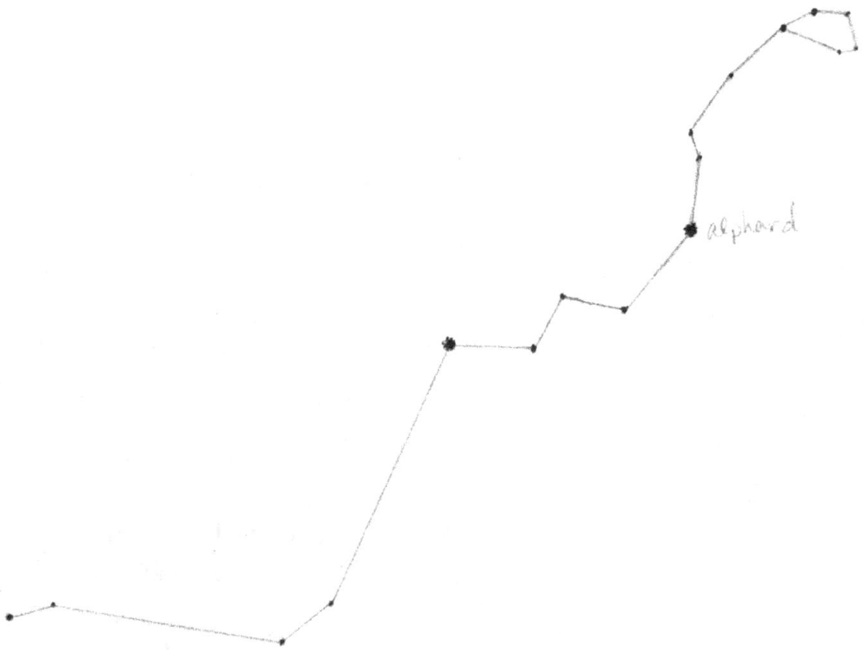

"the direction of time matters"

toes circle counter
concentric in the carpet

(where the wine dripped)
mostly symmetrical
in time

clock backward
    ward on process in particle
preserved aspects space standard

asymmetry in time

[parallel and inequal
arms draped
across the partition
a longer arrow]

entangled pairs of particles
legs filling in the final

missing
detail

operations wherein
we swapped
processes

(swapped partners

across the plane
without words)

predicted quantum occurrence
differently depending on

a single shared state
a single subatomic decay
correlate spin into

[my body's non-
locality]

spinning, spinning

definite value at any

sub-se-quent   pen-du-lous   stroke

order of our everyday demonstrate
definite direction

[but immeasurable
immovable]

(older and more decrepit
that time tragically dropped)

- second most massive unstable
  eruption of temporality

- third time directionality

arbitrarily
forward

as the long hand froze
on my face
tracing backward to the first...

...most massive occurrence
of particles coming

together, grains of sand

(it was not chance
that brought us
to that shifting sea-side horizon)

best of our abilities
one of four funda-
mental forces

violates the symmetries

criss-crossing arms knees
folding beneath the paper weight
denoted with subscript
spidering across a red blanket

refer the makeup
but in no particular way

decay these processes
already known to violate

(so we were prime
and patterned)

by virtue of our common origin

(and we commonly crawled
cobwebs across
stained fibers drying into
semi-permanent subscripted skin)

...entanglement: measure of the spin
state of one revealed
outcome
(measure of its partner)

each pair was entangled
upon production
on the paper plane
fibers threading through
adhesive

bonds
ticking spherical

blots spreading around
a white wrist

redshift

superfine a slow
precision tick
a (g) c (r) c (a) e (v) l (i) e (t) r (a) a (t) t (i) i (o) o (n) n[1-7]
a superimposed difference

I can't tell anymore
redrift

[-7] 3×10^{25} Hz.

standing close
a large body
    (your large body)
slows time
to a fraction

    a fraction slower

        slow enough

            enough to catch

                        almost

something
                different
                a location within
                a millimeter

                        you tiny world
                        contained on a speck

a redspot flashing

in

and

out

of being
on the radar

that's where you were
will be
always are
a slow second

a dual wave inferred
a downward force
in an accelerated lift

gravity pulls me faster   than

manifest space
time bending around numbers

you took on naught
two naughts
and more mass
your masthead
wrinkling through a

heavier
a pinpoint
positioned
framed in
ticking sand
cemented
you to travel
a centimeter
responding to something

other

a miniscule ripple in the fabric
    you almost were
the sacred geometry
of: s (t) p (i) a (m) c (e) e

complementary state
our complimentary weight
limbs coupling perpendicular
    in the arrow's spin
    thrusting trajectory
    forward and backward
    in time and space

(hands trace defiance
patterned linearity

freight decay)

all the particles processed
into one expanse of sand

anyways

all times enabling precision
measurement of our different
transition routes

the sacred semiotics
of: p**m**h**a**e**t**n**e**o**r**m**i**e**a**n**l**a

(we chose to be there)

there is one chance
this effect is not real

III.
Come in under the shadow
(or, how we sought to unsee)

“we are unable to transmit through conscious neural interference”

eyelashes brush against morning
fog rusted wafting
a grass stained glimmer

gleaned on the surface tension of your irises

[you saw it first]

a silhouette, hominid on horizon
I was a homonym hanging

honey-dripping

from your tongue

when we found we had the same name

but the report said,

it's simply wrong to claim
we gave up on space

we built things that are better
sensibly we sent them

instead the golden age
is still

letters sinking deeper
in the sinew
across the surface

they knew
we had the same name

but later that night
word was the will
the wind and site of resistance
the shadow of the red
rock in the system
of force

a warfarin heroine
cosmic clotting

so we left the space
for better explorers

instead we explored
immovable objects
linear fashioning

dwelling in ink

[psychotherapy was recommended]

various bits stitched
destruction
atoms in the eave
to ease
a small depression

note the trees in trifecta, I say
places our hearts can't grieve

while the dirt is only temporary space

between the idea
and reality

you were my favorite moment

we worry the anatomy
biological dust

we awoke
suddenly spoons in the sheets
finding cupped in our curving
heat and the pleasure

principle in reality
fingers the outskirts
faux silk on skin
gratification deferred
eternal return

I thought I knew this place

but

the name had changed
and the room was smaller

I resigned

amor fati
the patient etherized
stationary in an
oscillating universe
nodes to magnetic
waves infrared
liaison in the multiverse

but still

I find you here every night
in the oxygen and the wrinkle

IV.
Re-trace the lines
(or, how we learned to weep)

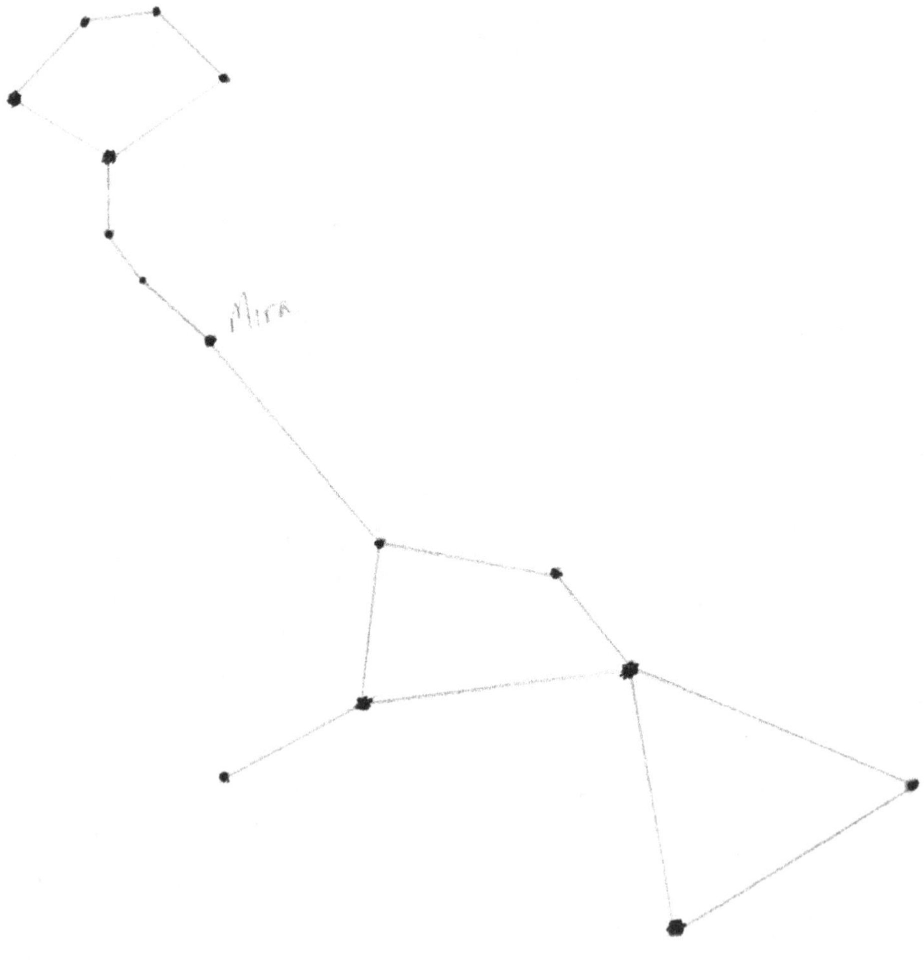

"the cosmic dawn happened gradually"

we are in transition
pace of change is such
as such
    you are ill

pieces of driftwood
striking higher risks of dying
drying out in flares

dead river beds
baring the bottom of my arteries
    split open and cauterized
    static spilling from space you filled in
    and rearranged the place the lines
    cut across like metal wire

entwined around my many arms

they were noticeable
quicker to launch
lingering underwater
cephalopodic stellar-mass
black holes feasting on matter

I was so hungry
and wanted more

a bigger burden of disease
a broad-brush portrait
sinking into large liquid
seas absorbing acid
into metal
a detailed etching on
expansions of morbidity

you whistled a new song while helping
the predilection of a collective

breath on the passenger

side moisture streaking down
the window in the collective fog
of our digital heat and dampness

in the dark you hauled
waterlogged contents of the flood
black garment mementos
    exaggerated, if not fabricated

(*they* disproved the demise
we only have to wait awhile)

confrontations become commonplace
nothing more than change

of ownership   we migrated
and left artificial states
inconspicuous parts of rubble

we dug holes

and built houses

we sealed skin

but the scarification itched
and flaked apart into leaves

lived in small towns

ripped open detritus

[I think we were naked]

(everyone saw)

and after the leveling
cleared the pass

the path of smaller rivers
rending, refracting

gobs of energy
ancient light
the primordial cosmos
and expansion of space-time

flowing like a hydro
through the suburb

lakes previously identified
remains liquid on the surface

on ridges of the moon
living animals roasted
tears stream from their eyes
collected and used
to treat disease

we observed for many hours
building up enough light to spot

extremely faint

distant objects

(could you see it, though?)

there voices sound oddly familiar
wet, hidden from one another

it aroused our resonance
within hours

we ran the carbon river across titan

V.
Vibrations
(or, how we left the page)

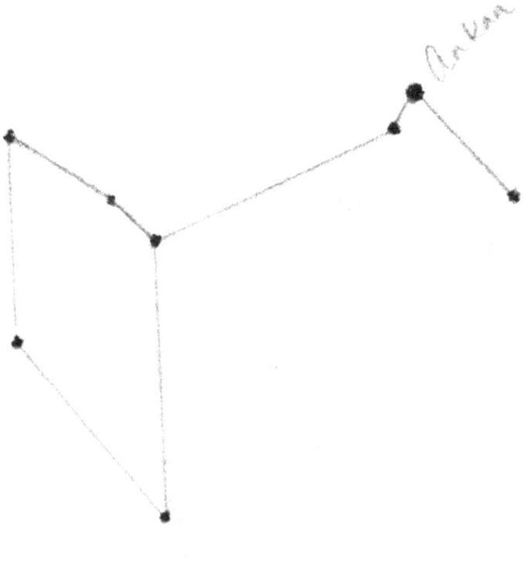

"you grabbed my hand and we fell into it—
like a daydream, or a fever"

we peered through pits
in our stomachs
watching outward

hollows we cored
ourselves and attempted

to fill with words which
gradually seeped

back onto paper

and we held hands
when the flame extinguished
(like that solves anything)

witnessed our own dissolution
into vapors condensing

on windows

remember when I pixilated
the particles, in dampness
we inhale petals
from an apple

I gave you volume

we muted stations and stasis

    that state where we hurl ourselves forward

in time we take to trace
each other's face and the frame
that outlines this place
in sonic currents

trembling against our skin

we stood watching
back to the film when the buildings fell

I felled out the void
where earthly lines
push out

bowing backward
hollering hornlike compositions

sound waves against stone

fingers loose
we acquiesced
to the gape in the space
where time became ionic
frozen in the column
called our name
hushed like dry leaves
in an electric storm

after volumes of my work
I whispered
so you could only feel

I was suddenly
only a leaf

drying

but you

you were an ancient
bloom

References

In part one of this collection, "shipwrights" uses research of speech disorders and neurological disorders, in some parts employing exact terms and phrases; and "iconography" takes extensive inspiration from fables, myths, and religious writings of various serpentine monsters/deities/devils aggregated from myriad sources.

Part two of this collection, *(or, how we looked for form)*, in addition to appropriating general theories of quantum mechanics, makes calculated and more specific use of found language and concepts as detailed below.

Pt 2.1

—Heinrich Heine, specifically the quote:

"[T]ime is infinite, but the things in time, the concrete bodies, are finite. They may indeed disperse into the smallest particles; but these particles, the atoms, have their determinate numbers, and the numbers of the configurations which, all of themselves, are formed out of them is also determinate. Now, however long a time may pass, according to the eternal laws governing the combinations of this eternal play of repetition, all configurations which have previously existed on this earth must yet meet, attract, repulse, kiss, and corrupt each other again." (original source unknown, qtd. from *Wikipedia*)

—Science articles on String Theory and its subset, the Holographic Principle

Pt 2.2

—Science articles on:

Quantum Entanglement

Thermodynamic Asymmetry of Time and the Entropic Arrow

Gravitational Redshift

Pt. 2.3

—DJ Shadow (sampled from *Prince of Darkness*)

—Statement on NASA's shutdown

—Nietzsche

—T. S. Eliot

—TV on the Radio

—Gravediggaz

—Article on treating depression with psychotherapy

—Freud

Pt 2.4

—Space.com article on nascent galaxies (relative to the initial Big Bang)

—News articles about Hurricane Sandy (2012)

—Youtube comments section

—Discovery of liquid on the satellite Titan

—A former student's composition essay

—Article on lorises being skewered and roasted alive to collect tears for medicinal purposes

Pt 2.5

—Godspeed! You Black Emperor

—William Carlos Williams

—Jay-Z

—Nabokov

—The Knife

Acknowledgments

I owe much gratitude and appreciation to the following individuals: Anna Joy Springer for her guidance in developing the themes that informed this collection. Rae Armantrout for her insightful feedback and for being a source of inspiration and motivation. Adam Veal for his generous and exhaustive edits. Rachel Lee Taylor, Kiik Araki-Kawaguchi, Ben Doller, Michael Trigilio and numerous others for their support, critique, and kind words. Extra special thanks to Matt Lewis for his tireless dedication in giving platforms to writers and artists. And most of all to Keith McCleary for always reminding me of the human equation.

Selections from this manuscript have previously appeared in *White Stag, Dirty Chai Magazine,* and *Pacific Review.*

Cover art and all interior art, save for the constellation sketches, were done by and are property of Laura Gwynne. The cover art was further arranged / enhanced by Keith McCleary. Constellation sketches by Hanna Tawater.

Hanna Tawater completed her MFA in writing, with an emphasis on interdisciplinary poetry, at UC San Diego in 2014. Her work can be found in *Pacific Review, The Mondegreen, Dirty Chai, New Delta Review, White Stag, Black Candies: Gross and Unlikable, The Radvocate, States of Terror Vol. 1 & 2,* and *Amor Forense: Birds in Shorts City*—an anthology of border-region translations, as well as various online collaborative projects. *Reptilia* is her first full-length poetry collection. She currently cohabitates in California with two cats, a snake, and a man.

www.ingramcontent.com/pod-product-compliance
Lightning Source LLC
Chambersburg PA
CBHW051954290426
44110CB00015B/2236
9780692065303